7/06
5

JUV/E8
GV
878.4
.B83
2003

WALKER

Chicago Public Library

R0401264910
World Series heroes

# A Note to Paren

W9-BBD-064

DK READERS is a compelling pr[...] readers, designed in conjunction w[...] experts, including Dr. Linda Gambrell, director of the Eugene T. Moore School of Education, Clemson University, and past president of the National Reading Conference.

Beautiful illustrations and superb full-color photographs combine with engaging, easy-to-read stories to offer a fresh approach to each subject in the series. Each DK READER is guaranteed to capture a child's interest while developing his or her reading skills, general knowledge, and love of reading.

The four levels of DK READERS are aimed at different reading abilities, enabling you to choose the books that are exactly right for your child:

Level 1–Beginning to read
Level 2–Beginning to read alone
Level 3–Reading alone
Level 4–Proficient readers

The "normal" age at which a child begins to read can be anywhere from three to eight years old, so these levels are only a general guideline.

No matter which level you select, you can be sure that you are helping your child learn to read, then read to learn!

LONDON, NEW YORK, MUNICH,
MELBOURNE, AND DELHI

**Senior Editor** Beth Sutinis
**Senior Art Editor** Michelle Baxter
**Publisher** Chuck Lang
**Creative Director** Tina Vaughan
**Production** Chris Avgherinos

**Reading Consultant**
Linda Gambrell, Ph.D.

Produced in partnership and licensed by
Major League Baseball Properties, Inc.
**Vice President of Publishing**
Don Hintze

Produced by
**Shoreline Publishing Group**
**Editorial Director** James Buckley, Jr.
**Art Director** Tom Carling,
Carling Design, Inc.

First American Edition, 2003

04  05  10  9  8  7  6  5  4  3  2
Published in the United States by DK Publishing, Inc.
375 Hudson St., New York, NY 10014

Copyright © 2003 DK Publishing, Inc.
All rights reserved under International and Pan-American Copyright
Conventions. No part of this publication may be reproduced, stored in
a retrieval system, or transmitted in any form or by any means,
electronic, mechanical, photocopying, recording, or otherwise,
without the prior written permission of the copyright owner.

Published in Great Britain by Dorling Kindersley Limited

A catalog record is available from the Library of Congress.

0-7894-9252-0 (PB)
0-7894-9546-5 (HC)

Color reproduction by Colourscan, Singapore
Printed and bound in China by L Rex Printing Co., Ltd.

Photography credits: All photos courtesy Major League Baseball
Photos and the National Baseball Hall of Fame and library except:
AP/Wide World; 12-13, 14, 26, 39; Corbis/Bettman: 27.

Discover more at
www.dk.com

# Contents

**DK** READERS

READING
**3**
ALONE

MAJOR LEAGUE BASEBALL™

# WORLD SERIES HEROES

Written by James Buckley, Jr.

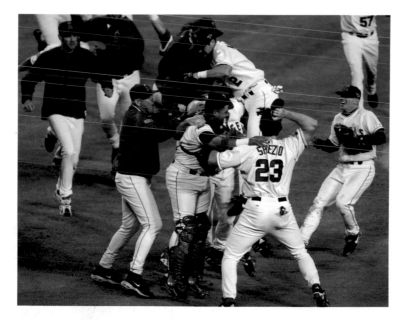

DK Publishing, Inc.

Walker Branch
11071 South Hoyne
Chicago, IL 60643

# A century of Series

Every baseball player dreams of being a World Series hero. From kids playing in the park to veteran Major League stars, everyone dreams about their team winning it all.

In 2003, the World Series celebrates its 100th birthday.

*Great pitcher Cy Young helped Boston win the first Series.*

R0401264910

The first World Series was played in 1903. The American League (A.L.) was only two years old that year. The National League (N.L.) had been around since 1876. At first, some N.L. teams didn't want to have a championship series with the new kids on the block. But team owners knew that fans wanted to see the best play the best every year.

Since then, in October, the A.L. champs have faced the N.L. champs in the World Series, which is sometimes called the Fall Classic.

*Troy Glaus of the Anaheim Angels was a 2002 World Series hero.*

Every World Series has created new heroes for fans to love. Sometimes the hero is a pitcher who blows the ball past an opposing team. Sometimes it's a slugger who blasts a dramatic, game-winning home run. Sometimes a player becomes a hero by making an awesome defensive play.

*Derek Jeter of the New York Yankees is a modern Series hero.*

**Play? No way!**
In 1904, the New York Giants won the N.L. title. Manager John McGraw refused to play the World Series because he thought the A.L. was too new!

For all those players, the dream came true. The moment they had wished for since they were kids had arrived. They had come through and helped their teams win.

This book tells the story of the greatest World Series heroes in the first century of the Fall Classic. Sometimes World Series heroes are the famous players fans talk about all the time. But occasionally, a World Series star is an everyday player who, at just the right time, becomes a hero.

# Heroic homers

Nothing in baseball is more dramatic than a home run in the World Series. A big Series homer thrills everyone— except the opposing pitcher!

Long-ball tales start with the most famous baseball player ever: Babe Ruth.

Babe hit 15 homers in seven Series with the mighty New York Yankees. His most famous homer came in 1932. Babe was playing against the Chicago Cubs. After taking two strikes, he pointed to centerfield. Then he slugged the next pitch right where he had pointed!

Did Babe "call" his shot? Some people are sure he did. Others say he was answering jeers from the Cubs. No one will ever know for sure, but it was one of the most famous home runs of all time.

*New York Yankee Babe Ruth was a World Series hero.*

*Bill Mazeroski celebrates!*

Another famous home run was not hit *by* a Yankee, but *against* the Yankees.

The 1960 World Series between Pittsburgh and New York went to Game Seven. The Pirates scored five runs in the bottom of the eighth to take a 9–7 lead. The Yankees struck back with two runs to tie the game.

Pirates second baseman Bill Mazeroski led off the bottom of the ninth inning. Bill was known for being a great fielder, but not much of a hitter. He stunned the hometown crowd and the Yankees by slugging a home run!

The Pirates won the game and the World Series! It was the first time a player had won the Series with a homer. The Yankees' Mickey Mantle had three homers in that Series. His 18 career Series homers are the most ever.

*Mickey Mantle helped the Yankees win seven Series.*

Some World Series home runs create pictures that live forever. One of these homers came in Game Six of the 1975 World Series.

The game was already a classic as it headed into extra innings. The Cincinnati Reds and Boston Red Sox battled back and forth in front of the fans at Fenway Park. Boston catcher Carlton Fisk led off the bottom of the twelfth inning. He hit the second pitch toward Fenway's famous leftfield fence. Fisk watched the ball sail

*Carlton Fisk says, "Go fair! Go fair!"*

*Joyous Red Sox players greeted Fisk (27) at home plate.*

toward the foul pole. He waved his
arms, cheering the ball on. It landed
fair—a home run! The Red Sox won
the game!

Two years after Fisk's famous homer, Reggie Jackson of the New York Yankees made baseball history.

*Mr. October, Reggie Jackson, slugs his third homer in 1977.*

In Game Six of the 1977 Series against the Dodgers, Reggie earned his famous nickname: "Mr. October." The World Series is almost always played in that month.

In the fourth inning, Jackson hit the first pitch he saw from Burt Hooton for a two-run homer. In the fifth, he did it again. He clubbed Elias Sosa's first pitch into the rightfield seats. It was another homer and two more RBI.

More than 56,000 fans were on their feet in Yankee Stadium and millions more watched at home as Reggie led off the eighth inning. Incredibly, he once again hit the first pitch he saw for a home run! Three pitches, three homers! Thanks to Mr. October, the Yankees won the game and the World Series.

There is a famous baseball saying: "It only takes one." That means that no matter how bad the situation is, it just takes one key hit to make a difference.

In Game One of the 1988 World Series, Dodgers outfielder Kirk Gibson "got one" and made the most of it. He had to overcome an injury to do it.

*All eyes were on the ball as Gibson's homer flew out.*

**Heading west**

Kirk Gibson played for the Los Angeles Dodgers. But from 1890 to 1957, the team played in Brooklyn, New York, and was called the Brooklyn Dodgers.

Though he had a badly hurt leg, Kirk pinch-hit with two outs in the bottom of

the ninth. His team trailed by one run. He was their last hope. Ace A's reliever Dennis Eckersley was on the mound. On a 3–2 pitch, Gibson somehow slugged a a game-winning, two-run home run!

During Game Six of the 1991 Series, Twins fans in the leftfield seats got a great show. First, Kirby Puckett made an amazing catch right near them.

Later, in the 11th inning, with the scored tied 3–3, Kirby thrilled them again. The noise in the Metrodome was deafening as Puckett came to the plate. He smacked a homer that sailed right over the spot where he had made the catch earlier. The homer won the game!

*Kirby yells for joy!*

Remember Bill Mazeroski and his surprise homer? In 1993, Toronto outfielder Joe Carter matched Maz's feat. The Blue Jays were

down 6–5 against the
Philadelphia Phillies in the
bottom of the ninth in Game Six.
Carter smacked a dramatic
three-run homer to win the
game and the World Series!

*Joe Carter was only the*
*second player ever to hit a*
*Series-winning homer.*

The New York Yankees have won more World Series titles than any other team. Their list of World Series batting heroes is a long one, from Babe Ruth to Mickey Mantle to current star Derek Jeter.

*Scott Brosius watches his dramatic homer soar into the night.*

In the 2001 World Series against Arizona, the Yankees made heroes and history. In Game Four, Tino Martinez's two-run homer in the bottom of the

*Tino Martinez*

ninth tied the game. Then Jeter won the game with another homer in the 11th.

In Game Five, amazingly, the Yankees did it again! They trailed in the bottom of the ninth and once again hit a clutch homer. This time, Scott Brosius's long ball tied the game. Arizona went on to win the Series, but the Yankees had the homer heroes.

# Pitching aces

Ever since the World Series began 100 years ago, fans have argued about one thing, Which is more important: good hitting or good pitching? The heroes in this section know the answer to that question. They are the greatest pitchers in World Series history.

*Christy Mathewson*

In 1905, New York Giants superstar Christy Mathewson achieved a feat that will probably never be matched. In six days, he pitched three

*Babe Adams*

shutouts and had 18 strikeouts. His earned run average (ERA) was 0.00 and he only walked one batter!

Four years later, Babe Adams of the Pittsburgh Pirates nearly matched Christy's feats. Only a rookie, Babe won three games to help Pittsburgh beat the Detroit Tigers. In Game Seven, he pitched a shutout against the Tigers team that included future Hall of Fame outfielder Ty Cobb.

*Lew Burdette celebrates in 1957 with his teammates.*

Almost half a century after Christy and Babe won three Series games each, Lew Burdette did it, too. Sometimes one pitcher can just take over a Series. Lew did just that against the mighty Yankees in 1957.

Lew was not the pitching ace of the Milwaukee Braves. Lefty Warren Spahn was the big star. In the Series, though, Lew came through. After winning Game Two, he pitched shutouts in Games Five and Seven. For the Series, his ERA was a terrific 0.67.

While Mickey Mantle and Yogi Berra were the Yankees' hitting stars in the 1950s and 1960s, Whitey Ford ruled the mound. The lefty holds career World Series records for wins (10) and games pitched (22). He helped the Bronx Bombers win six World Series titles.

*Whitey Ford*

*Don Larsen fires a pitch in the only perfect Series game.*

Though Whitey Ford was the star, the Yankees did have other pitchers. One was Don Larsen, who had an amazing moment in the spotlight.

In 1956's Game Five, Don threw the only perfect game ever in a World Series! A perfect game is when a pitcher does not allow any batters to reach base.

There have been only 16 such games in baseball history!

Sandy Koufax of the Dodgers is considered one of the best pitchers ever. In the World Series, he won four games while helping the Dodgers capture World Series titles in 1963 and 1965.

*Few things in baseball were harder to hit than Sandy Koufax's fastball.*

Pitchers like Larsen and Koufax always expected to finish what they started. Most modern pitchers, though, need relief pitchers to finish up their games.

In Game Seven of the 1991 World Series, the only way the Twins were going to get starter Jack Morris off the mound was with a crowbar!

*Jack Morris starred in 1991.*

The game was a real thriller. Neither the Minnesota Twins nor the Atlanta Braves could score in the first nine innings. Jack was mowing down Braves batters inning after inning. During the regular season, Twins manager Tom Kelly might have pulled Morris to start the tenth inning. Not in the World Series, though. Big Jack toughed it out and pitched a perfect tenth.

Then his teammates finally helped him out, scoring in the bottom of the tenth to win the Series!

**Babe the pitcher?**
Believe it or not, Babe Ruth was a World Series pitching star, too! He pitched for the Red Sox in 1916 and 1918. He set a record by not allowing a run for 29 innings in a row.

The World Series can be the place where a great star finally gets to shine. Lefthanded ace Randy Johnson is one of baseball's all-time best pitchers. He is the winner of five Cy Young Awards, the second most in baseball history. But Johnson had learned to hate October because he had had little success in postseason games.

Randy was determined to change his fortune in the 2001 World Series against the Yankees. In Game Two, he pitched a gem of a game, a three-hit shutout for the Arizona Diamondbacks.

In Game Six, Randy's teammates made it easy. They beat the Yanks 15–2. Randy shut down New York again. The Series was tied at three games apiece. Coming up was the crucial Game Seven.

*Randy Johnson is one of the hardest throwers in baseball.* 31

As if having Randy wasn't enough, Arizona was blessed with Curt Schilling. The hard-throwing righthander was Arizona's starter for Game Seven. Curt had already pitched brilliantly for the Diamondbacks. He had won Game One 9–1. In Game Four, he was winning until the Yankees made an amazing comeback (see page 21).

*Curt Schilling and teammate Randy Johnson made for a great one-two pitching punch.*

*Randy and Curt display Arizona's trophies in 2001.*

In Game Seven, Curt battled
Yankees ace Roger Clemens inning after
inning. Curt left the game in the eighth.
Following another reliever, guess who
came in? That's right…Randy Johnson.
Though he had pitched the night
before, he came in with the game on the
line and held the Yanks scoreless.
Arizona won in the bottom of the ninth,
Johnson had his third win of the Series!

*Hard-throwing reliever Mariano Rivera is the best ever.*

All of the pitchers we have met so far are starting pitchers. However, in the pressure of the World Series, relief pitchers often play key roles.

No relief pitcher has had more success in the World Series than the Yankees closer Mariano Rivera.

In five World Series, Mariano has been almost unhittable. He holds the all-time record with eight saves. In 27 innings, he has a tiny 1.67 ERA and 25 big strikeouts.

In 1998, he had saves in three of the Yankees' four victories. He was the 1999 World Series MVP with two saves and a win. Mariano saved the day!

*Rivera jumps for joy!*

# Defensive wizards

Time to check out the third key part of every baseball game: defense. Some players have become baseball legends because of their glove work in the Series.

In 1955, Sandy Amoros of the Dodgers made a catch that saved a Series. He caught Yogi Berra's long drive to left with two men on, keeping the Dodgers ahead in Game Seven. Brooklyn won the game and their first Series.

### Home park

Ebbets Field in Brooklyn was home to the Dodgers. Sadly, the classic old ballpark was torn down in 1960.

*Game saver! Sandy Amoros snags the ball just in time.*

To this day, one famous World Series defensive play is called simply "the Catch." Ask real baseball fans who made "the Catch" and they'll say, "Willie Mays!"

In Game One of the 1954 World Series, the super-fast New York Giants outfielder took off when he heard the crack of the bat. Cleveland's Vic Wertz had smashed a long drive to very deep centerfield.

Mays flew back toward the wall. With his back to home plate, he reached up and snagged the ball! Then, in one motion, he spun and threw the ball back in, holding the runners on base. It is still thought to be the finest catch of all time. The Giants went on to win the Series in four games.

*First, Mays made this amazing catch. Then he whirled around and fired the ball back in.*

In the World Series, infielders usually make news only when they make an error. The pressure of being in the big games sometimes makes even good players make mistakes.

But one remarkable pair of infielders didn't make any mistakes on their way to Series stardom.

*Brooks Robinson didn't let a little dirt get in his way.*

In 1970, Baltimore third baseman Brooks Robinson was a human vacuum cleaner. Against the powerful Cincinnati Reds, Brooks made several awesome defensive plays. He made diving catches, long throws, and stunning stops. His Orioles team won the Series in five games.

*Graig Nettles*

In Game Three of the 1978 Series, Yankees third baseman Graig Nettles was a one-man brick wall. He made four spectacular plays to rob Dodgers batters of hits. The Yankees won the game and the Series.

Third base is called the hot corner, but these guys were two cool customers!

# Angels in the Series

The stories in this book so far have been about individual heroes. We've met the players who stood out for their success in the biggest games of all—the World Series.

In 2002, the baseball world watched in amazement as a new champion was crowned. In a twist, instead of having just one hero, the Anaheim Angels were made up of an entire team of heroes!

*Edison Field dressed up for Game One in 2002.*

The Angels have been around since 1961. Until 2002, however, they had never won it all. They had never been to a World Series, though they had come close several times.

The Angels (sometimes called "the Halos") faced the San Francisco Giants, led by Barry Bonds. Each team won two of the first four games. For the Angels, rookie pitcher Francisco Rodriguez was a big surprise, helping in both Angels wins. Angels sluggers Tim Salmon and Troy Glaus chipped in with homers. First baseman Scott Spiezio had several key RBI.

*Troy Percival saved three games for Anaheim.*

The Giants still had punch, however. In Game Five, they stomped on the Halos 16–4. In Game Six, they led by five runs in the seventh inning. It looked like the Angels' dreams would die again.

Then, the Angels all became heroes. Spiezio hit a key homer. Darin Erstad got another. Little shortstop David Eckstein had some key hits.

*After 10 years as an Angel, Tim Salmon finally got a ring.*

The Angels closed the score to 5–4. Then in the bottom of the eighth inning, Glaus smacked a two-run double that gave the Angels the lead! It was one of the most amazing comebacks in Series history. Troy Percival came on to slam the door on the Giants.

The hero parade continued in Game Seven as rookie pitcher John Lackey held the Giants. Outfielder Garret Anderson whacked a three-run double for the lead, and Percival shut the door again. A team of heroes were the champs!

*Anaheim Angels win! Let the celebration begin!*

New World Series heroes are made every year. They hit, pitch, play defense, and make comebacks. Will you be one?

# Glossary

**ace**
A nickname for a team's top starting pitcher.

**American League (A.L.)**
One of two groups of teams that make up the Major Leagues.

**Bronx Bombers**
A nickname for the New York Yankees. The Bronx is a section of New York City.

**closer**
Nickname for a pitcher a team depends on to finish a game, often in tight situations.

**crucial**
Something that is very important.

**earned run average (ERA)**
A statistic used to measure the success of a pitcher. It means the average number of earned runs he allows in nine innings.

**error**
When a fielder makes a mistake on a catch or a throw, allowing a batter to reach base or a runner to advance.

**extra innings**
If a game is tied after nine innings, the game continues with extra innings.

**foul pole**
Tall metal stakes in each outfield corner that mark the limits of the playing field. Oddly, a ball that hits the foul pole is a fair ball.

**mound**
The raised pile of dirt on which a pitcher stands to throw to the batter.

**most valuable player (MVP)**
An award given after each season and after each World Series to the player or players who have contributed the most to their teams' success.

**National League (N.L.)**
One of two groups of teams that make up the Major Leagues.

**perfect game**
A game of at least nine innings in which the starting pitcher does not allow any batters to reach base.

**postseason**
A name for the parts of the baseball season that come after the regular season.

**reliever**
A pitcher brought in after the starting pitcher. Also called a "relief pitcher."

**save**
Usually, a pitcher who finishes a game that his team wins after he comes in with men on base is said to have "saved" the game. He receives a statistical credit. There are other situations, too, in which a pitcher can receive a save.

**shutouts**
When a team does not allow the opponent to score any runs in a game.